PLAYGROUND AND TEENSPEAK

Abson Books London
First published August 2007
© Michael Janes
Cover design Chris Bird

Printed by Gutenberg Press, Malta
ISBN 13 9 780902920 90 3

PLAYGROUND SLANG AND TEENSPEAK

compiled by Michael, Daniel & Leah Janes

ABSON BOOKS LONDON
5 Sidney Square London E1 2EY
Tel 020 7790 4737 Fax 020 7790 7346
email absonbooks@aol.com | web www.absonbooks.co.uk

INTRODUCTION

This little book is for everyone – kids and young people who want to be sure there isn't a word they've somehow missed and grown-ups who want to try and understand just what it is the 'yute' are saying.

As with all underground language, Playground Slang and Teenspeak serves as a protective barrier that prevents outsiders (adults in this instance) from prying into the user's world and helps to reinforce the user's identity as a member of a group or culture, perhaps injecting a feeling of pride as well.

Included are words for different social groups (chavs, pikeys etc) and subcultures (emos, goths etc) as well as relating to the online community of video gamers, 'h4x0rs' (hackers) and 'leetspeakers', 'roffling' away in front of their screens.

Youth can be embarrassingly truthful so, if the description fits, they won't hesitate to call someone a 'crater face' or 'tank ass' or maybe even a 'BOBFOC' or 'ginger minger'.

Aware that language and slang are forever changing, it is not claimed that this little book is fully comprehensive but, hopefully, it contains enough of a sample to interest, intrigue and enlighten.

Michael, Daniel & Leah Janes

–age	suffix added to a noun for emphasis, e.g. *I got lots of partyage this weekend!*
air	(a) used when someone is ignored, e.g. *I got air* (b) rubbish, no good, e.g. *he's air*
allow!	forget about, don't bother with, e.g. *allow him, man, he's chatting breeze!*
allow that!	(a) who cares about that!, leave it out! (b) yeah, OK
arsed	bothered, e.g. *I can't be arsed*
awesome	amazing, excellent

bagsey, bugsey	claim something you want
bait	blatantly obvious, e.g. *it was so bait he wasn't gonna come*
ballin'	living the good life and showing off how rich you are
bang	have sex with
banged up	(a) imprisoned (b) beaten up (c) high (on drugs) (d) stupid, ridiculous, e.g. *that's a banged up idea!*
bare, bares	(a) very, e.g. *that test was bare hard* (b) lots of, e.g. *there are bare mandem there*
batty boy	male homosexual
beef	(a) grudge, e.g. *you got beef with me?* (b) fight, e.g. *you better not start a beef with me*
big up	(a) praise, e.g. *I wanna big up my friends* (b) thank publicly

blad, bled, blud	friend
bladdered	drunk
blank	ignore, e.g. *she completely blanked me*
blates	yeah, definitely
bling-bling	showy gold or diamond jewellery
blinged up	wearing loads of bling-bling
blood	close friend (from 'blood brother')
BOBFOC	'Body Off Baywatch, Face Off Crimewatch', used to describe someone with a great body but an ugly face, e.g. *she's a real BOBFOC*
boff, boffin	clever person
boyed	humiliated, e.g. *I got boyed*
brainfart	when you've forgotten what you're saying, e.g. *sorry, I had a brainfart*
brainiac	clever person, often used to mean the opposite, e.g. *great idea, brainiac!* (from Superman comic strip)

brap!, brapp!	used after a word or phrase to indicate approval, e.g. *I just got paid, brapp brapp!*
breadbin	humorous way of saying 'bredrin'
bredrin	friend or friends (from 'brethren'), e.g. *wagwanin, ma bredrin?*
brick	(a) shit yourself with fear, e.g. *I nearly bricked it* (b) very cold, e.g. *it's brick out there*
brill	great, cool
bro	friend
bubblin'	excited
buff, buffting	good-looking, e.g. *she's well buffting*
bum chum	male homosexual
bum fluff	wispy, sparse hair on the face
butters, butt ugly	very ugly

CBA	'Can't Be Arsed'
chav	young working-class person, often aggressive, usually wears designer-style clothes, tracksuit, trainers and fake gold jewellery
cherps, chirps	chat up, flirt with
cherry picker	guy who likes sex with virgins
chill, chill out	relax
chillax	calm down, relax (from 'chill' & 'relax'), e.g. *hey, dude, chillax!*
choong, chung	very attractive
class	excellent
confuzzled	confused and puzzled
convo	conversation (in instant messaging), e.g. *I'm having a convo on MSN*
cool	(a) good, great
	(b) impressive, awesome

	(c) relaxed, laid-back
	(d) stylish, classy
cotch, kotch	(a) relax, chill out
	(b) hang out or stay somewhere, e.g. *where ya cotchin' tonight?*
crater face	face with bad acne
creps	trainers
crew	group of friends
crib	house, home
crusty	dirty, yucky, e.g. *a crusty old bag lady*
cuss	swear, swear at

da	the
dat	that
dis	this

diss	show disrespect to, insult, e.g. *are you dissing me?*
div, divvy	stupid person, e.g. *that ain't what I mean, you div!*
dork	stupid or uncool person
drunk-dial	make a phone call while drunk, e.g. *he's always drunk-dialling me*
dude	(a) guy, person (b) friend
durbrain	stupid person
dweeb	clumsy moron

emo	(a) type of punk rock music (aka emocore) known for its 'emo'tional lyrics (b) subculture spawned by emo music

(c) member of the emo subculture. The stereotypical emo is sensitive, has long hair over the eyes, an unfair reputation for self-harm and, when called an emo, will insist that he or she is not an emo

ends (a) money (from 'dividends')
(b) neighbourhood, e.g. *I'm reppin' my ends*

Facebook (a) use Facebook, a college social networking site, e.g. *I've been Facebooking*
(b) check out or stalk someone using Facebook
fit good-looking
fly cool, attractive
freak (a) weirdo
(b) disreputable person

fudge	low grades in an exam (F U D G and E refer to GCSE grades), e.g. *I'm going to get fudge in my exams*
fugly	extremely ugly

G

gangsta	(a) type of rap music (b) young person who listens to gangsta rap and is associated with the urban underworld. The typical gangsta wears baggy trousers, a hoodie and trainers
gay	(a) not very good, e.g. *that show was a bit gay* (b) unfair, e.g. *mum won't let me go out, she's being gay* (c) not working, e.g. *I can't go online, the computer's being gay*
gaylord	idiot
ginger minger	redhead (offensive term)

(all 'g's pronounced as in 'got')

ginger ninja	redhead (term of endearment)
goth	(a) type of music related to punk rock
	(b) subculture spawned by goth music
	(c) member of the goth subculture. The typical goth wears black clothes and pale make-up, is quite solitary and is fascinated by the macabre
grindin'	working very hard

h4x0r	(a) hacker (in gamer language)
(pronounced hacker)	(b) someone showing great skill at a game
happy slapping	slapping or punching someone randomly and photographing it on a camera phone
hard	tough, e.g. *my brother's well hard*
heavy	cool, great
hench	big strong man

hickey	love bite
hood	neighbourhood
hoodie	(a) hooded sweatshirt
	(b) person in a hoodie with the hood up (seen as troublemaker)
hype	(a) excited, e.g. *he's all hype*
	(b) really cool

ice	diamonds, jewellery
innit, init	(a) used instead of isn't it, e.g. *that's your teacher, innit?*
	(b) used instead of yeah, e.g. *I'm coming home, init*
innit like, init like	used for emphasis or to express displeasure, e.g. *you're well late, innit like!*

J

jack
(a) steal, e.g. *someone jacked my phone*
(b) rob, e.g. *I got jacked*

jokes
(a) funny or fun, e.g. *that film was jokes*
(b) the same as 'just kidding',
e.g. *Craig asked me out – **Really?** – Jokes!*

j00 (pronounced you)
you (spelling used in chatrooms and video game forums), e.g. *ha! I pwn j00!*

K

kev another word for chav

kicks trainers, shoes

kotch see cotch

kthxbye, kthnxbye (pronounced 'k, thanks, bye')
used for ending online convos abruptly, often shows annoyance

laters		see you later, e.g. *laters, dude!*
lawl		sarcastic form of 'lol', used after someone has made an unfunny joke
leetspeak (also l33tspeak, 1337speak, 13375p33k or just 1337)		type of communication in chatrooms where user replaces many letters with numbers
like		word inserted as a filler, e.g. *it was, like, well good!*
lol		'laughing out loud', used online usually when you have nothing else to say
long		(a) boring, time-consuming (b) difficult (c) taking a long time to do something, e.g. *he's bare long*
lurgies		imaginary germs, e.g. *don't touch him! he's got lurgies!* (used by young kids)
lush		(a) good-looking (b) cool, great

Maccy Ds	McDonald's
mandem	(a) men, people, e.g. *there are bare mandem over there*
	(b) friends, members of a gang, e.g. *all da mandem will miss ya*
manky	bad, disgusting, e.g. *what's that manky smell?*
mardy	sulky, grumpy (North of England & East Midlands)
massive	(a) really good, e.g. *a massive party*
	(b) crowd, gang, e.g. *say hello to all da massive*
McPee	go for a McPee: pop into McDonald's to use the toilet
mega	(a) great, good, e.g. *he's mega, your blad*
	(b) very, really, e.g. *that's mega awesome*
meh	(a) used for showing indifference, e.g. *wanna see a film? – Meh*
	(b) so-so, average, e.g. *that game was a bit meh*

merk	(a) beat up
	(b) kill
metal mouth	person with braces on their teeth
minge	pubic hair
minger	(a) really ugly person, especially a girl or woman
(rhymes with singer)	(b) smelly person
mingin'	(a) ugly
	(b) disgusting
	(c) smelly
mint	great, brilliant, e.g. *that's well mint*
MSN	Microsoft® instant messaging application for chatting online
muff	hairy vagina
muffed up	messed up, screwed up
munch	snacky food
munter	ugly female

my bad	admission of personal fault or mistake
MySpazz	(a) MySpace, a popular social networking site
	(b) use MySpace, e.g. *what are you doing? – Oh, I'm MySpazzing*

nab	arrest, e.g. *I got nabbed by the popo*
nang	cool, good
ned	Scottish word for good-for-nothing, stupid or aggressive person (similar to chav)
–ness	suffix added to a word for emphasis, e.g. *we've had six hours of schoolness*
newbie, newb	someone new to a game, forum etc
n00b	(a) someone annoying who is new to a game
	(b) stupid person who thinks they know everything

nuff	(a) plenty of, enough
	(b) very
numpty	silly idiot (used in Scotland)

oh noes!	used for showing dismay
ohnosecond	moment of panic when something bad has happened or a mistake has been made
oi oi!	innuendo when mention of dating or sex, e.g. *I'm seeing Jess tonight – **Oi oi!***
OMG	'Oh My God'
OMFG	OMG, with addition of the f-word
own, 0wn, pwn	(a) beat, humiliate, e.g. *you pwn3d me in Halo 2!*
('pwn' and 'pwn3d' are	(b) do really well, e.g. *I completely owned that test*
pronounced 'pone' and	(c) win, e.g. *I owned at Grand Theft Auto*
'poned' and are written this	(d) get or be owned: be humiliated,
way in video game forums)	e.g. *you got owned!*

ownage	(a) humiliation, e.g. *it was bare ownage when he fell down!* (b) excellent, e.g. *that party was ownage*
pants	rubbish, e.g. *that film's pants!*
pikey	(a) lowlife, e.g. *they're thieving pikey scum!* (b) traveller, gypsy (offensive term)
plastic	(a) superficial, obsessed with appearances, e.g. *she's so plastic* (b) fake girl from privileged background (from the film Mean Girls)
playa (pronounced 'player')	guy, good with girls and with more than one girlfriend
poo	rubbish, e.g. *that lesson was a bit poo*

	popo	(a) policeman
		(b) police
	pwn	see own
Q	**quality**	really good, e.g. *your homework's quality*
R	**rad**	really cool (from 'radical'), e.g. *that gig was so rad!*
	random	weird, unexpected, e.g. *that's so random!*
	randomer	a stranger
	rank	disgusting, smelly
	rare	(a) unpleasant
		(b) ugly
	reachin'	going to a place, e.g. *are you reachin' dat club?*

rep	show off the fact of belonging to a particular area, group etc, e.g. *I'm reppin' SE14, man!* (local areas are often given as postcodes)
retard	person of low intelligence (not PC)
rinse	(a) play repeatedly, e.g. *that tune's getting rinsed like anything* (b) beat, humiliate
roffle	(a) used for conveying laughter, e.g. *I fell off my chair – Roffle* (b) laugh, e.g. *I roffled out loud*
rofl	'rolling on the floor laughing', used in chatrooms and forums (often tongue in cheek) when someone has said something funny
roll deep	hang out with a large group of people, e.g. *me and the crew are gonna roll deep tonight*
rudeboy	(a) someone who listens to ska music and often wears chequered clothes (Jamaican term)

(b) person, mainly from a poor background, into Afro-Caribbean or African-American culture
(c) tough guy, considered worthy of respect

sad	(a) uncool, unfashionable
	(b) nerdy and boring,
	e.g. *you're sad, you collect stamps!*
	(c) pathetic
sad act, saddo	uncool, nerdy or pathetic person
safe	(a) cool, good, OK
	(b) reliable, e.g. *da mandem say yo is safe*
	(c) hi (greeting)
	(d) sure thing,
	e.g. *wanna come to my house? – **Yeah, safe!***
safeting	(a) good, e.g. *yeah, man, it's safeting!*

	(b) definitely, sure thing
scally	another word for chav (used in Liverpool)
scene	(a) general term for music subculture, e.g. *the emo scene*
	(b) derogatory term for follower of subculture for fashion reasons, e.g. *look at her, she's so scene*
scenester	follower of music trends just because they are fashionable. The typical scenester has dyed hair, wears a ratty T-shirt and has lots of friends on MySpace
shout, shout-out	used by DJs to show respect, e.g. *a big shout-out to all my mates!*
shut up!	used for showing shock or disbelief (not to shut someone up), e.g. *Jake passed his exams – **Shut up!***
sick	really cool, e.g. *your new bike is sick*

sket	slutty girl
snog	kiss
soz	sorry, e.g. *you stepped on my foot – Soz!*
space cadet	strange or distant person, as if on another planet, possibly because of drugs
spasticated	stupid, retarded (not PC)
spaz	(a) idiot, e.g. *stop acting like a spaz!* (not PC)
	(b) go wrong, stop working, e.g. *my computer is spazzing!*
spit	rap, e.g. *I'm gonna spit some rhymes*
square	clever person who, for this reason, is uncool
standard	(a) another way of saying 'of course'
	(b) normal, regular, e.g. *he's standard*
sup	what's up? (greeting)
sux0r, suxx0r (pronounced suck-zor)	(a) someone who sucks at (is bad at) a computer game etc

(b) something that really sucks,
e.g. *revision is the sux0r!*

T

tank ass	big bum
teh	the (in internet forums and video game applications)
testiculate	wave your arms about while talking bollocks (from the words 'gesticulate' and 'testicles')
tight	(a) close, e.g. *they're really good friends, they're tight*
	(b) cool
tings	(a) things
	(b) sex, e.g. *I got ma tings last night*
townie	another word for chav
tru dat	sign of agreement, e.g. *she's so buff* – **Tru dat**
twoc	nick, steal (from 'taken without owner's consent'), e.g. *some pikey twocked my dad's car*

	uber	(a) really, super, e.g. *uber cool*
		(b) great, awesome

wagwan	hello (a corruption of what's going on?)
wagwanin	what's going on?, e.g. *wagwanin, bled?*
wasteman	waste of space, useless person
well	very, e.g. *that's well good!*
whatever	used for suggesting you're not interested or you don't care, e.g. *I went to a disco last night – **Whatever***
w(h)iz, w(h)izz	urinate
wicked	really good, e.g. *a wicked film*
w00t	shout of joy (supposedly from 'we owned the other team' from its use in video game forums), e.g. *w00t! I just passed my GCSEs!*

wordage	(a) use of words, e.g. *cool wordage, man!*	
	(b) words	
wuss	wimp, weakling	

ya	(a) you	
	(b) your	
yard	home, house, e.g. *I'm cotching down my yard today*	
yo	(a) hi (greeting), e.g. *yo, what's up?*	
	(b) your	
	(c) you	
yute	youth	

IDIOMS

am I bovvered?	I don't care
be down with	like something or someone or understand them, e.g. *I'm down with that*
brother from another mother, sister from another mister	expression for a close male or female friend
chat breeze	talk a lot of rubbish, e.g. *that don't make sense, you're chatting breeze, man!*
chill your beans!	calm down!, relax!
get down with	(a) get on someone's good side and be accepted into their confidence, e.g. *I think our politicians should get down with the yute*

	(b) understand, e.g. *get down with the lingo, man!*
	(c) have sex with
give me some skin!	used when greeting friends by slapping or touching the palm of your hand against theirs
kissing your teeth	kissing sound made by scraping tongue against upper teeth, a sign of disdain equivalent to saying 'tut tut'
naa mean?	know what I mean?
out of order	used about someone or their behaviour that is unacceptable or wrong, e.g. *he was well out of order*
pop your cherry	lose your virginity, e.g. *he popped her cherry*
shit a brick	be really scared or upset

so's your face, **so's your mum**	reply to anything considered an insult, e.g. *you're pants – **So's your face!***
talk to the hand 'cos the face ain't listening	used when not wanting to listen to what someone is saying, combined with the gesture of a raised palm
your mum!	(a) insulting reply when not wanting to give an answer, e.g. *what's your name? – **Your mum!*** (b) used by itself as a general insult

OTHER TITLES AVAILABLE

Language Glossaries

American English/English American
Australian English/English Australian
Irish English/English Irish
Gay Slang
Geordie English
Lancashire English
Rhyming Cockney Slang
Playground Slang and Teenspeak
Home Counties English

Scouse English
Yiddish English/English Yiddish
Scottish English/English Scottish
Yorkshire English
Prison Slang
Hip Hop English
Rude Rhyming Slang
Military Slang

History

The Death of Kings
A history of how the Kings & Queens of England died

Literary Quiz & Puzzle Books

Jane Austen
Brontë Sisters
Charles Dickens

Gilbert & Sullivan
Thomas Hardy
Sherlock Holmes
Shakespeare

All of these titles are available from booksellers or by contacting the publisher.